ILLEGAL

WITHDRAWN
Seeking the American Dream

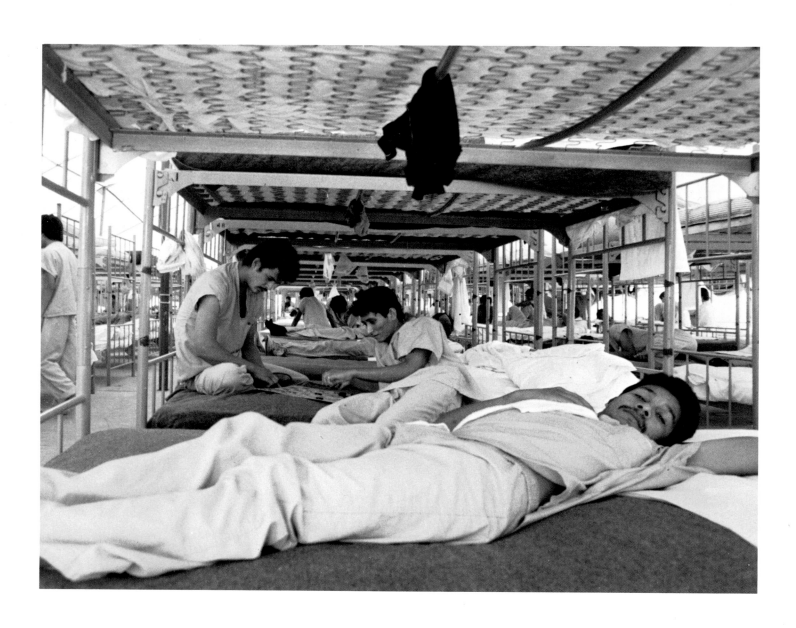

ILLEGAL

Seeking the American Dream

Photographs and Text
by
Phillip Anastos
and
Chris French

RIZZOLI
NEW YORK

This book is dedicated to the great human spirit the world over, and the pursuit of freedom, happiness, and a better way of life—against all odds.

Phillip Anastos

Chris French

First published in the United States of America in 1991 by
RIZZOLI INTERNATIONAL PUBLICATIONS, INC.
300 Park Avenue South, New York, NY 10010

Library of Congress Cataloging-in-Publications Data
Anastos, Phillip.
    Illegal: Seeking the American Dream: eyewitness report
and photographs/by Phillip Anastos and Chris French.
        p.   cm.
    ISBN 0-8478-1367-3
    1. Lower Rio Grande Valley (Tex.)—Emigration and
immigration—Pictorial works. 2. Aliens, Illegal—Texas—
Lower Rio Grande Valley—Pictorial works. 3. Teenage
immigrants—Texas—Lower Rio Grande valley—Pictoral
works. I. French, Chris. II. Title.
F392.R5A53   1991
305.9'0693—dc20   90-29070
                                             CIP

Printed and bound in U.S.A.

Contents

FOREWORD

Refugees are not traditional migrants. Refugees are people who flee violence and persecution—and fleeing is not easy.

The decision to abandon one's homeland is always a difficult one. In the case of Central American refugees, it is one that involves a combination of push-and-pull factors. The last dozen years have produced a long list of evils that have contributed to pushing Central Americans out of their homes: widespread human rights abuses, including torture and "disappearances," chronic civil war, and targeted violence by death squads, as well as economic disarray caused by insecurity and destruction.

Even in the worst of circumstances, it is never the majority that flees; most people hunker down and try to ride out adversity. Fleeing involves leaving behind home, family, culture, country. It often involves physical risk and danger, and it involves becoming a stranger, confronting the unknown. A person must place extraordinary value in his life and future, or those of his children, to risk flight.

Refugees are not foolish; they usually make choices that are well considered and that they believe are in their own or their family's best interests. Thus, the place to which they flee is a pivotal issue. For many refugees, a desire for peace, freedom, and opportunity for prosperity pulls them towards the United States. The very essence of what Americans believe the United States represents—freedom, liberty, and opportunity—precipitates that pull. It is we who put the words on the Statue of Liberty, "Give me your tired, your poor, your huddled masses yearning to breathe free. . . . Bring these tempest-tossed to me. I lift my lamp beside the Golden Door."

But, as pointed out to me by a Salvadoran refugee living in the United States, the Statue of Liberty faces east, not south. And in recent years we have not welcomed refugees from near our shores with the generosity that has characterized our response to refugees from distant points in Europe and Asia. In the period from 1983 through 1990, the Immigration and Naturalization Service (INS) approval rate for asylum seekers from El Salvador, Guatemala, Haiti, and Honduras was under 3 percent; excluding these four nationalities, the approval rate for all other nationalities during this period was 35 percent.

Denial of asylum only tells part of the story of the poor reception given by the United States to asylum seekers of these nationalities. Only relatively few Haitians have managed to reach our shores to claim asylum; the overwhelming majority—more than twenty-two thousand during the 1980s—has been interdicted by the United States Coast Guard on the high seas and returned, denied any meaningful opportunity to pursue asylum claims. Central Americans have been detained and routinely coerced into abandoning their asylum claims and opting for "voluntary departure." In 1988 a federal judge ruled that "INS agents used a variety of techniques to procure misrepresentations." Judge David Kenyon said that Salvadorans were "intimidated or coerced to accept voluntary departure even when they had unequivocably expressed a fear of returning to El Salvador." The average of four hundred and fifty Salvadoran deportations and required departures per month in the mid-1980s represents only the tip of the iceberg: the INS did not keep a count of the number of "voluntary" departures.

"This conduct is not the result of isolated transgressions by a few overzealous officers," Judge Kenyon observed, but rather "results from INS policies...approved, authorized, and/or ratified by INS personnel at all levels." There is hope for the 1990s, however. Congress has recognized these abuses and created a "temporary protected status" for Salvadorans starting in 1991. A class-action suit brought on behalf of Salvadorans and Guatemalans forced the INS in December 1990 to agree to reconsider as many as one hundred and fifty thousand asylum cases denied during the 1980s and to affirm that foreign policy, ideological beliefs, and broader enforcement considerations are not relevant to determining refugee status.

The failure of the 1980s, in many ways, has been a denial of our self-image, a negation of our espoused ethic. Sometimes, in ignorance, we who are among the world's most fortunate look at others and depersonalize them. We see a crowd, a mass, a horde; we speak of "them." Yet, in better moments, we recognize each refugee as a person, worthy of dignity, a member of a family, someone's child.

That recognition of the human story is the value of *Illegal: Seeking the American Dream*. The photos taken by Phillip Anastos and Chris French help us to refocus on the individual refugee within "the refugee problem." We see each one's hurt, fright, hope, joy. These photos also help us to see ourselves, how we as a people are responding to these strangers who seek to be among us.

This is not a book of abstract photography. It depicts real, flesh-and-blood people; it concerns the core of the American ethos. Despite all the welcome some Americans provide, this book shows we have a good bit of work to do in the decade ahead to live up to our self-image.

Roger Winter
Director
United States Committee for Refugees

NOTE ON THE PHOTOGRAPHY

There are many dilemmas faced by a photographer when first approaching a story, but two elements are most important: what am I trying to show and how am I going to show it?

The first question involves the role of the photographer. As a young man starting out in the news business during the 1960s, I was constantly admonished to "be objective."

That's something I have wrestled with throughout my professional career. It sounds good, and the concept is right. There is, however, one problem with the theory—photographers are human, and humans are not objective creatures. We love, we hate, and we get involved. *Illegal* could not have been done without emotional involvement. This does not mean, though, that it is a dishonest effort. The compassion and sensitivity shown by the photographers make it work.

The second question is how to illuminate the subject. These photographers chose black-and-white film to do the job. Black-and-white photography is a medium shorn of frills and distractions. It is content over color. A decision I made when I became President Ford's official photographer was to shoot in black and white. There were many reasons for this, not the least of which was the ability to use available light. That essentially meant I was able to shoot pictures without a flash. A flash disturbs your subjects, and the attention suddenly shifts to the photographer, not to those he is trying to capture on film in their natural habitat. It's the "fly-on-the-wall" approach. The photographer and his camera become part of the woodwork to produce photos of events as they really happen. Ideally, he sees events unfold as they would had he not been there.

The pictures in this book are remarkable not so much for their technical ingenuity, but for what they show. They were taken from the heart. They propel us to the very center of the young immigrant's world.

They are fresh and inquisitive and were taken with a kind of wide-eyed naïveté, as if the photographers had awakened in the middle of someone else's nightmare. Many of them are straightforward shots of young people looking right into the camera. You would think they were posing for a family snapshot. Some are smiling, some are not. All of them are in the custody of U.S. authorities. These photos are reminiscent of the work of Lewis Hine, among the most influential photographers ever to use his camera in the cause of social reform. His pictures of the young, the poor, the immigrant, and the worker of the early 1900s were a tribute to Hine's belief that photography is a vehicle to inspire and to communicate.

What is inspirational to me in particular is the fact that Phillip and Chris have chosen a path away from the more selfish and negative influences of our society and instead used their ability and enthusiasm to do something positive. They have given a human face to people who are generally ignored.

Illegal is a project born of social conscience. It is impossible not to feel what they felt and to see what they saw. This is the highest form of journalism. One of the ironies of this book is that one doesn't have to travel the world to produce dramatic photos of human suffering. As these young men have proved, they can be taken right here in our own backyard.

David Hume Kennerly

INTRODUCTION

Throughout our high school years we studied photography and participated in our school's photography exhibits. In the spring of 1989, as we searched for a new project, we read that an unprecedented number of children from Central America were illegally crossing the border into Texas. Referred to as "unaccompanied minors" by U.S. immigration officials (since they arrive without family or friends), these children, mostly boys between the ages of thirteen and seventeen, are fleeing their homelands to escape the government and opposition forces that are drafting young men for military service at younger and younger ages. These unaccompanied minors pose many problems for the U.S. government, chiefly where they should be housed and how they should be treated. Further, when these children turn eighteen they must be considered adults. This means they must be moved to a detention center. From there more than 95 percent of them face deportation. They will be returned to their "homeland," where their safety cannot be guaranteed, and where they almost certainly face a very dangerous future.

We knew we'd found our subject.

After convincing our families to let us travel to south Texas during our summer vacation, we set out in June 1989 for the Rio Grande Valley.

We flew to Houston, then made the long drive to Brownsville, a town hard by the Rio Grande, the natural border—and barrier—between the United States and Mexico. Brownsville also is the crossing point of choice for thousands upon thousands of refugees, not only from Central America but from as far away as Eastern Europe and China.

The Brownsville–Harlingen area is one of the poorest stretches of towns in the United States, yet we were struck by the contrasts. We'd expected a brown, barren landscape crosscut by a big, muddy river and its shallow canyons and washes. And in part it is like that. But there also are patches of green, lush fields and shade trees. Sometimes it's just a matter of which side of the river you're on.

Unlike other entry points into the United States, in south Texas all refugees are confined to the Brownsville–Harlingen area, "the Valley," while waiting for their applications for asylum to be processed. The Immigration and Naturalization Service (INS) started this policy in December 1988, due to the flood of "illegals" into the area. The policy change states: "All asylum requests should be adjudicated by the office of original jurisdiction." The purpose is to make quick determination of requests for asylum.

Before the INS changed its policy, fewer than 1 percent of refugees remained in the Rio Grande Valley. They usually traveled on to major cities on the eastern seaboard, and their cases were reviewed by INS officers in those cities. There they had a much better chance of finding legal help and support. But now that has changed. The refugees in south Texas are denied the rights that other illegal aliens receive; that is, to leave the area, to go to school, or to find a job while waiting to apply for refugee status.

If an illegal alien is eighteen or older and traveling without a family, he or she is put into a detention center. This amounts to being locked behind barbed wire or bars, guarded, required to wear an orange prisonlike uniform, and marched from place to place. Limits are imposed on recreation, seeing loved ones, and even on personal hygiene. Most of these people really don't understand what is happening to them; our asylum policies and procedures are extremely complex and change frequently. Few of these detainees ever manage to be represented by legal counsel, since the detention centers in south Texas are in remote areas where few immigration attorneys are available.

In an effort to maintain the family unit, families who cross the border illegally are taken to Red Cross shelters rather than to detention centers. The Red Cross accommodations are simple but pleasant, and the atmosphere is relaxed. These detainees are permitted to wear street clothes and wander about the town during the day, if they choose. The children can play, and there are activities and classes in English for everyone conducted by Red Cross volunteers who seem genuinely caring. This "soft" detention is in stark contrast to the treatment at the detention centers.

There are also government-run homes for unaccompanied minors—by far the best places we visited. One had a backyard pool, another a volleyball court and comfortable furniture. The children receive medical checkups and immunizations, are allowed to go on field trips to such places as the town library, and spend several hours a day in the classroom learning English. They are even taught how to do practical things that will enable them to make their way in the United States. The staff tries to reunite these children with relatives already in the United States and to develop lists of foster families, though there are never enough of these families available. These unaccompanied minors are even provided with legal assistance.

Yet these children are still trapped—almost as much as the people who fill the detention centers. They've left their homes fearing for their lives and come to the United States in desperate need of safe haven. But, because they enter America along the banks of the Rio Grande, they usually face deportation to a place where their safety cannot possibly be guaranteed. It's little wonder that many people say the word *unfair* doesn't seem adequate here.

In April 1989, members of the U.S. Committee for Refugees (USCR) made a fact-finding trip to the lower Rio Grande Valley for a firsthand look at the processing of refugees who were being detained after crossing the border there. Perhaps their report offers some of the best answers as to why refugees are treated differently there than in other areas of the country. The report states: "The presumption evident at every level of the INS—with some noteworthy individual exceptions—is that asylum seekers from countries in our own hemisphere are overwhelmingly economic migrants and that their claims to refugee status are, with few exceptions, baseless." The members of the USCR also came back from their visit "convinced that Central Americans and Haitians face a *presumption of ineligibility* for refugee status by U.S. immigration authorities." In truth, as the USCR team concluded, "The United States is deporting people seeking refuge to countries where their safety cannot be guaranteed—and to which they are afraid to return. That is an unacceptable, inhumane practice."

We went to south Texas in search of a story—and we found one. Cameras in hand, we shot pictures, we talked, we asked questions, we wrote, and we shot more pictures—over three thousand in all—hoping to capture in the faces the emotion and the story of what was happening to these unfortunate people. We followed the border patrol—searching the fields, patrolling the river, and picking up "illegals" along the way. At

Red Cross shelters in Brownsville and San Benito we listened to families huddled together, wrapped in their dreams. At the Port Isabel Service Processing Center the story became one of men and women lost in despair with nowhere to turn. In Raymondville and Los Fresnos we saw groups of unaccompanied minors waiting apprehensively, hoping to get a fresh start in life. And what we learned above all from our visit to south Texas was that if these undocumented aliens knew their rights and could be assisted, they might apply for asylum or other forms of legal relief that they are entitled to. Instead, they sit in confinement with little or no understanding of what is happening to them. Here is their story.

Many "illegals" hope this is their last view of America from the outside. In this case, someone took his belongings in hand to cross the river, leaving a suitcase behind. On the other side of the Rio Grande is Brownsville and the symbol of "freedom"—the American flag flying in the distance.

THE BORDER PATROL
Welcome to America

"Illegals" already within the United States are the responsibility of the United States Border Patrol. At the Brownsville, Texas, station, the agents—forty of them— are responsible for patrolling the area from the mouth of the Rio Grande up to San Pedro, a distance of about seventy-four miles. They provide round-the-clock coverage. Some of the agents work on horseback (a daytime assignment), others work on foot, but most patrol the levees and surrounding terrain in off-road vehicles. They have the right to stop anyone on mere suspicion within twenty-five miles of the border.

Because it is impossible to patrol the entire jurisdiction effectively with the number of men available, the border patrol uses many types of sensors along the river, which help to detect the "illegals." And they have another distinct advantage: they know the area far better than the "illegals" do.

When "illegals" are spotted crossing the Rio Grande, the nearest border patrol agent is immediately summoned to the scene. The arrests are usually made without incident.

At one point the border patrol responsible for Brownsville was apprehending about two thousand "illegals" a week. When we visited, the number had dropped dramatically, to about three hundred and fifty, because the incarceration of people in the detention centers had started to deter illegal immigration. Many of the "illegals" crossing the border now are Mexican "commuters," people who cross daily to do menial jobs. The border patrolmen have the authority to determine the status of those they apprehend. If they consider their prisoners to be "commuters," they simply escort them to the border. The processing time for one of these "commuters" is between five and ten minutes, while a true illegal alien requires about three hours.

The border patrol's job is further burdened by its responsibility for catching drug smugglers entering the country, a small number when compared to the tide of illegal aliens. At the Brownsville station the agents are aided in their drug interdiction efforts by drug-sniffing dogs.

The border patrol is looked upon by some as the enemy. However, the agents are simply doing their job and trying to keep the number of refugees crossing the border to a minimum. Certainly, it is difficult to decide exactly what should be done, or who should be admitted. Yet the treatment these refugees face—parallel to that of common criminals—seems bewildering and unfair to them.

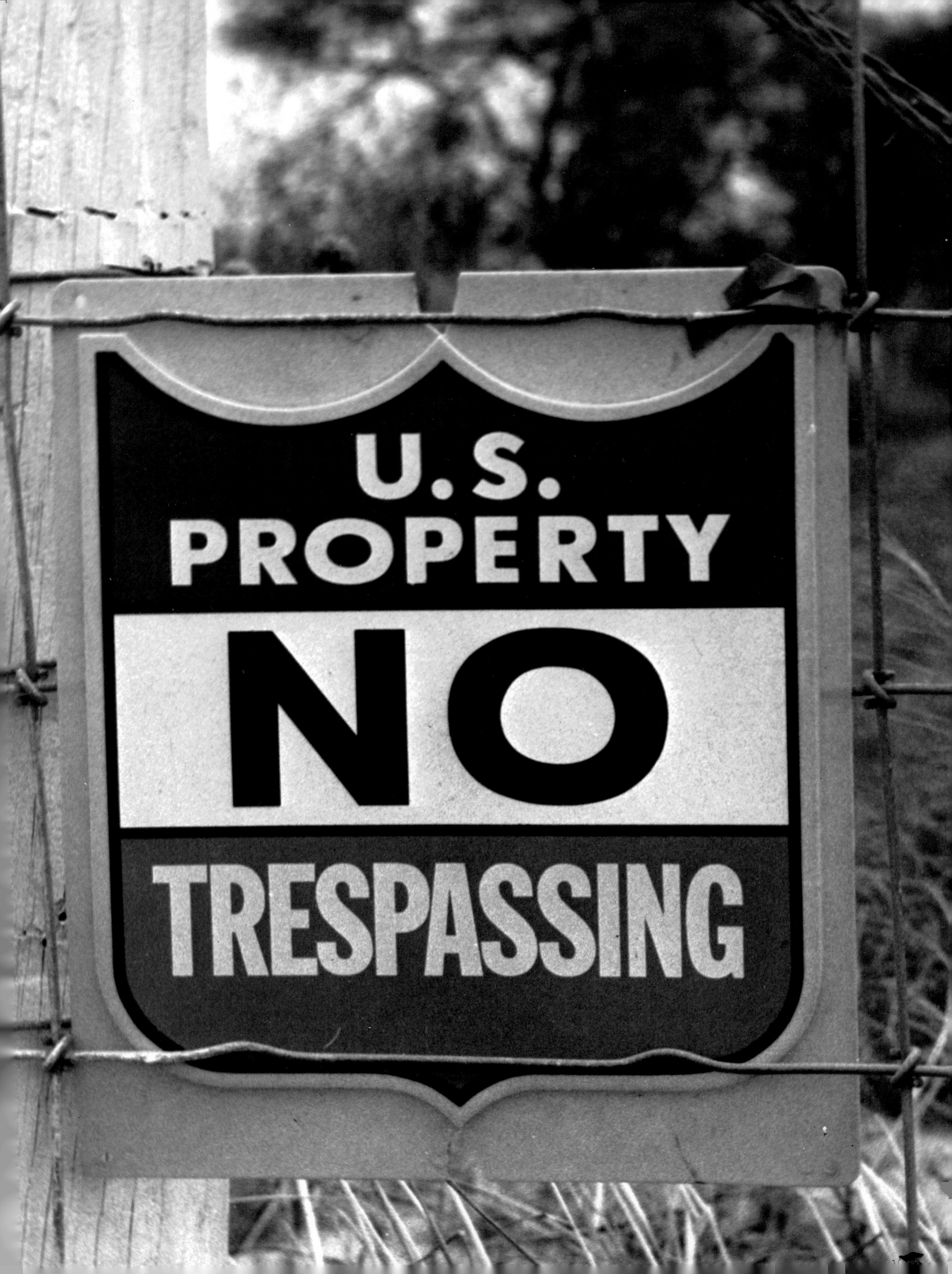
U.S.
PROPERTY
NO
TRESPASSING

The border patrol has the responsibility for patrolling the bridge connecting Matamoros, Mexico, and Brownsville, Texas. Patrol officers make sure that all those crossing have the legal right to enter the United States.

Border patrol agents, aware of the Rio Grande's popular crossing spots, patrol the river and surrounding areas around the clock. Many crossing points happen to be very tempting due to the river's low depth; but in fact fast currents make them extremely dangerous.

*It is almost impossible for the border patrol to
catch every "illegal" crossing the river. However,
agents meticulously search the surrounding areas
for any tracks or other clues.*

Overleaf:
Many of these desperate immigrants cross in broad
daylight, even though they are bound to be seen by
patrolmen.

Just after sundown is the most popular time to cross the border; although even then most "illegals" are immediately apprehended.

No match for the border patrol with its vehicle and searchlight, three Mexican youngsters are picked up in a field near the Rio Grande.

The Brownsville train yard is a popular refuge for "illegals." They hide under the halted trains and in the cargo cars, waiting for the next train heading north. Border patrolmen know when the trains are due to depart and patrol the yard at these times in order to catch the "illegals" trying to jump on to the trains and find a safe way out of Brownsville.

Border patrol agents survey not only the river valley but also the nearby towns. Within twenty-five miles of the border, agents have the right to ask anyone to show their papers at any time, even if they have not committed a crime.

Left and overleaf:
Trying to outrun the border patrol is virtually
impossible. Detainees are immediately searched
for weapons or drugs, and often handcuffed.

49

Several times during the course of a day, the border patrol brings "illegals" they have apprehended to an office where they are registered and processed—a long, tedious, and intimidating experience. They are then directed to one of the holding facilities, usually a detention center, a Red Cross shelter, or an unaccompanied minors home.

Only so many "illegals" can be processed at one time. The rest, including children, are usually put into a jail-like holding cell.

While many of the agents speak Spanish, the language barrier is yet another obstacle for most of the "illegals," who seem to be bewildered, even totally ignorant of what is happening to them.

UNACCOMPANIED MINORS
Kids Struggling Alone

We had to keep reminding ourselves that the unaccompanied minors were our age. Many of them come from countries ravaged by war. If that hasn't marked them, the journey to the United States, often hazardous in the extreme and filled with hardship after hardship, almost certainly has.

They flee from conditions we can barely imagine, and most of them would rather give up everything they know and everyone they love than be "drafted" into the dreaded military, whose troops march through the streets "cherry picking" kids and telling them they've just "volunteered" for the army. The guerrillas are no better, employing exactly the same tactics. A very real fear we heard voiced over and over was that you could end up fighting against your own brother!

Their families do try to help them. Money is hoarded so that one child might get to the United States and eventually send for the whole family. This is the dream to which they all cling.

If they make it to the Rio Grande and still have any money, they are often easy marks for *coyotes*, men who promise to get "illegals" across the river safely and, perhaps, even settled in the United States—for a sum, of course. As often as not, these rip-off artists take the kids' money and run.

Once an illegal alien has crossed the river, the chances of *not* being picked up by the border patrol or INS officers are slim. Security is such that it is virtually impossible to escape from the Rio Grande Valley.

Once apprehended, the "illegals" are sent to a home for unaccompanied minors (run by the Justice Department) as long as they are under age eighteen. Here they at least have a chance to be adopted or sponsored. A few turn up in Red Cross shelters, though these are intended for families with children. If they admit to being eighteen (and most do, since they've not had time to learn to navigate the system), they're placed in a detention center to be readied for deportation.

While in the unaccompanied minors homes we interviewed many refugee children. They hesitantly told us stories of their horrible journeys to the United States in search of a new chance in life.

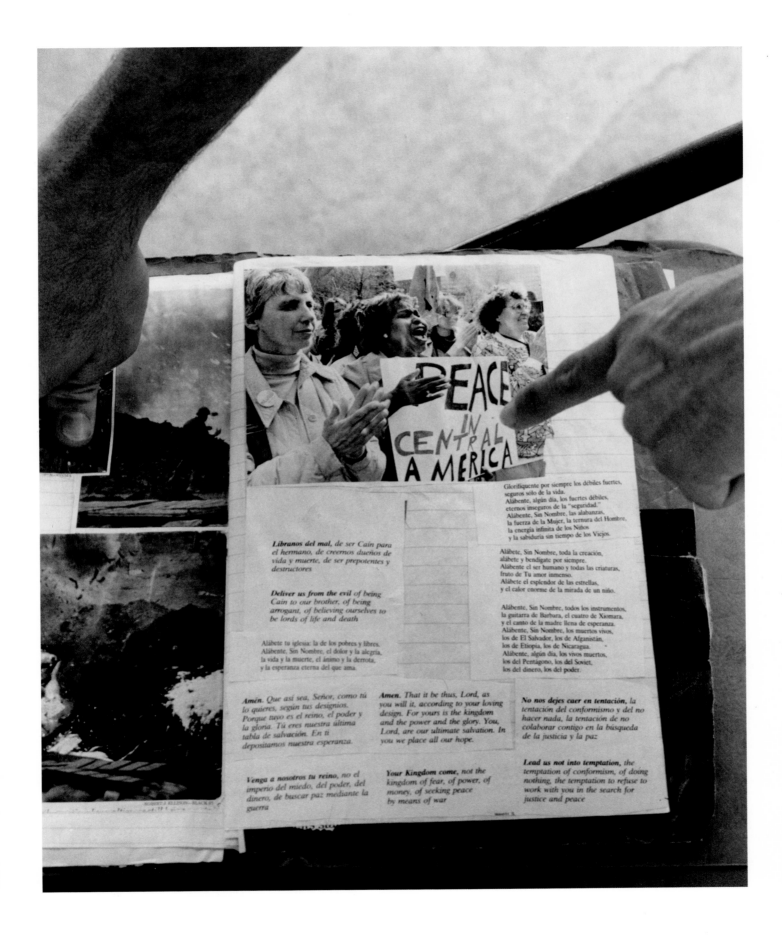

Some refugees carry scrapbooks full of memories
of their past and the violence they witnessed.

PEDRO

Two years ago Pedro forced himself to leave his family and home in Managua, Nicaragua. Like so many others we talked to, he was unwilling to join the military, where the only thing one can count on is being killed. Fifteen-year-old Pedro covered up his escape by telling people he was taking a trip to Matamoros, Mexico. In fact, he and thirty-two others boarded a bus that would take them away from their families and homeland forever. The trip took about a month, but when they arrived in Mexico they found trouble, not freedom. Pedro was harassed by the *Federales*, who took his money and the little food he'd brought and deported him to Guatemala. There he scrounged bits to eat and looked for places to sleep. He learned how to live one day at a time. He began to think he should have stayed in Nicaragua, that he missed his life there—until he thought about living in America. That dream drove him to return to Mexico.

Pedro found a job in Mexico, and his employer provided him with a place to sleep. For Pedro, life was suddenly pretty good, but he knew he had to move on. While considering the best way to enter the United States, he was told that if he swam across the Rio Grande and called for a taxi to take him to the church-run Casa Romero, he'd be safe.

He accomplished this, but now finds himself trapped. If he turns himself in, the INS will put him in a detention center as soon as he turns eighteen. He can't stay at Casa Romero forever.

SONIA

Sonia is sixteen years old. The threat of political violence at home in Progreso, Honduras, was constant, so her only choice was to leave. Traveling with her brother and sister-in-law, she worked her way to Guatemala and later to Mexico. They walked most of the way but managed to ride a bus through part of Mexico.

The trip through Mexico was punishing in every way. They found themselves without food, money, or anyone to turn to for help. The lack of jobs in Mexico made it extremely difficult to earn a living. They were lied to, and what little money they earned was taken by a *coyote* who told them he'd lead them all the way into the United States.

After a month of hazardous travel, they did make it across the Rio Grande into the United States, but they were picked up in a bus station by the border patrol. Sonia's brother and sister-in-law have already been deported, and she's in a home for unaccompanied minors. Sonia has relatives in the United States, but she has not been able to reach them.

RUTH

At seventeen, Ruth was forced to flee from her home, which lay in ruins, and from the military in Honduras. Her brother was a member of a group of insurgents, so no member of Ruth's family was safe. They scattered, leaving Ruth with no money and no place to stay. At a friend's home, Ruth was convinced that she should try to make it to the United States. Although her friend was not allowed to accompany her, the girl's older brother agreed to lead Ruth to the Mexican border. The two hitchhiked to the border, and then it was time for Ruth to walk on alone. Fortunately, she soon found a family who gave her food and shelter and directed her to what they considered the safest crossing point.

She walked many miles, but when she finally reached the crossing point it was full of *coyotes*. Alone, Ruth feared she might be raped. She quickly moved downriver and managed to cross into the border town of Laredo, Texas, on her own.

Ruth was captured almost immediately and taken to the border patrol station. She got into a Red Cross shelter in Brownsville, where she stayed for a week before being sent to a home for unaccompanied minors.

When we met her, she was still hopeful that a sponsor would be found for her, but time was running out; her eighteenth birthday was not far off—a day that should be a joyful celebration is for her, as it is for so many in her predicament, a dreaded date that signifies a move to a detention center and probable deportation.

REYNALDO

Reynaldo comes from San Miguel, El Salvador. At the age of thirteen he was forced to become a guerrilla. He carried an M-60 machine gun and had about twelve "men" under his command. Sent on a mission to destroy bridges in his hometown, he found he could not bring himself to do it and plotted an escape. He sent his own band of guerrillas off in one direction while he went in the other. Immediately, he headed to his mother's house—only to find his men there waiting for him.

On Christmas Eve he was able to escape again, this time with more success. Two weeks later, however, as he hid in the hills near his family's home, he could hear the guerrillas harassing his family. He knew that his father, mother, three sisters, and two uncles were at home. Then he heard machine-gun fire, followed by a loud explosion. When he reached his house, everyone in it was dead, his home destroyed.

Reynaldo lost his head. The friends who sheltered him put him in a straitjacket for three days to prevent him from taking his own life. When at last they could talk to him, they convinced him that his only hope for survival was to return to the military. He agreed, knowing their lives would be in danger if he refused.

Again he managed to escape, this time making it to Guatemala, hitchhiking a good part of the distance. There he became very ill. A woman took him in and spent three weeks nursing him back to health.

When he was well enough to travel, he hitchhiked to Guatemala City and finally made it into Mexico on foot. He spent forty-five days there, traveling across the country by train in an unorthodox and very dangerous manner: he clung to the outsides of train cars for long periods of time.

By the time he reached the U.S. border, Reynaldo was starving, so he took his chances and crossed the Rio Grande by day. Once across, however, he was unsure of the direction he should take until he remembered a trick his father had taught him when he was very small—throw your shoe in the air. Whichever direction the toe points is the way to go!

Reynaldo arrived in Harlingen, Texas, and went to the various churches in search of food. At some point he made a deal with an attorney, who eventually double-crossed him and turned him over to the authorities when Reynaldo could not pay him.

Reynaldo talks of his sleepless nights and the relentless nightmares of his family being murdered. He lives in a home for unaccompanied minors, but he is having trouble there because of what are termed his "attitude" problems. Soon he will be eighteen and will have to move to a detention center. His chances for adoption are slim, given his past.

EDGAR

Edgar is from Guatemala. At fifteen he escaped from his country, leaving behind his family, whom he doubts he will ever see again. The idea of being forced into the military was more than he could stand; he considered the trip to the United States the only answer.

Accompanied by a cousin, Edgar was on the road for one month, the journey made almost entirely on foot. In Mexico they found a family willing to feed and shelter them for one night. When they got to the U.S. border, they saw five Guatemalan boys who had been wounded by Mexican *Federales*. They knew they should wait until nightfall to make the crossing. Nevertheless, they were starving and scared of being attacked. Consequently, they plunged into the Rio Grande in broad daylight. As they reached the U.S. side, Edgar spotted a dead body on the bank. It hit him then just how easily his own life could have been taken.

Edgar and his cousin made it all the way to the United States, but they were caught by the border patrol soon after crossing the Rio Grande.

SANTOS

Santos is from Chinadega, Nicaragua, where his mother and ten brothers and sisters still live. His father died when he was very young. His mother sold drinks on the streets in order to bring in enough money, together with what the children earned, to support the large family. Eventually his mother started her own small business selling clothes.

When the Sandinistas came to power, they seized his mother's business. Most of the other children were self-employed, but Santos was in a difficult position since he'd not yet served his time in the military.

Santos and four other boys escaped by boat to El Salvador and worked there for nine months. From El Salvador they swam across a river to get into Guatemala, then "hitched" rides on trains by clinging to the sides or lying on top of freight cars to get into Mexico.

In Mexico they spent four months working in the fields and loading trucks, jobs that were very demanding physically. Santos and three others finally boarded a bus and rode to the Rio Grande. Only a fifty-yard swim stood between them and what they thought was freedom.

They chose to cross at two o'clock in the morning, under cover of darkness—and, they hoped, well out of sight of the border patrol. They made it safely and were at the point of congratulating themselves as they walked along a railway line when the border patrol moved in and picked them up. Santos still believes that if they hadn't been slowed down by one member of the group, who had a hernia and walked with great difficulty, they would have escaped detection.

Santos knows two people in the United States, an aunt in Miami and a friend in Washington. Lacking an education—he's had two years of school—he's not optimistic about his future and only hopes that "the generosity of the American people" will permit him to stay in the country. Ultimately, he wants to send for his family.

NOE

Noe is seventeen and from El Salvador. He's had nine years of schooling, significantly more than most Salvadorans. He fled from El Salvador to avoid the war, having no desire to serve on either side.

Leaving behind his parents, four brothers, and two grandparents, he set out with no money. He made it to the United States by himself, hitchhiking, walking, and begging. It took twelve days.

Noe's first priority is to get to New York, where he has an aunt. He wants very much to become a lawyer, but knows he cannot ask his family for money because they haven't any. He is having a hard time reaching his aunt, but the staff at the unaccompanied minors home is trying to help.

JOSÉ

Sixteen-year-old José is from Honduras. He told us his father had died "due to political problems." José believes his father may have been tortured. He lived with his grandmother from the age of seven, when his mother abandoned him to live in Miami. Like so many of the other young "illegals," José felt he had no choice but to leave Honduras. He certainly wanted no part of life in the military.

After bidding farewell to his grandmother and younger brother, he walked to neighboring Guatemala. There he caught a bus through the mountains to the Guatemala-Mexico border. He swam across a river and spent four months trying to find odd jobs—anything to earn a few dollars.

He paid a *coyote* to enter the United States, but the bus he traveled on was stopped by the INS. Since José didn't have papers, they held him for a couple of days before bringing him to the Red Cross shelter. He had been there three months when we visited.

HERNAN

Hernan, from the town of San Pedro Sula in Honduras, is seventeen. The youngest of seven children, he lived with his mother, a seamstress and telephone operator. He never really knew his father, who died when Hernan was very young.

Although Hernan worked as a mechanic to help support the family, he was not satisfied living in a place where the poverty would never go away, where he'd have no chance at all to prosper. One of Hernan's brothers had escaped to Germany, and he too wanted to get out to, as he says, "better my life."

Hernan's journey, however, would be not to Germany but to the "land of opportunity," the United States. His family had managed to save some money, so Hernan's trip was relatively easy. He was able to travel by bus all the way to Guatemala, a two-day trip. When he reached Mexico, he began to walk, resorting to bus travel only occasionally. The trip to the U.S. border took him a month.

Hernan reached the Rio Grande in March and crossed it alone, but he proved no match for the border patrol when they spotted him walking through a field along the river.

He says he has a cousin in El Paso and that he's been trying to reach her. Maybe he will.

WALTER

Fourteen-year-old Walter is from El Salvador. He and his mother traveled by bus to the Mexican border, which took two days. Then, after about three days of walking, riding on buses, hitchhiking, and begging for food, the pair reached Matamoros and crossed the Rio Grande into Brownsville, Texas.

In Brownsville they boarded a bus heading north. When the INS stopped and searched the bus, they picked up Walter and his mother and brought them to the Brownsville Red Cross Shelter.

Walter told us that he has a twenty-year-old sister in Houston and that they had been trying to reach her. She has been in the United States for four years, and he and his mother hope that with her as a contact, they'll be allowed to stay, but it is doubtful they will be able to find her.

FRANCISCO

Francisco is a seventeen-year-old Nicaraguan, who was taken from his homeland when he was a very small boy following a horrifying experience. A group made up of his family and their neighbors had gathered in the village square to talk about the problems facing them when, suddenly, troops arrived. Francisco's father, uncle, and grandfather were gunned down. Somehow, Francisco managed to escape. He was taken to Honduras, where a man cared for him for the next six years. When he was ten, the man abandoned him.

Francisco moved to Robatan Island, where he lived on coconuts and learned to bury himself in the sand to escape detection by bandits, who roamed the area robbing and killing. Eventually, he left Honduras for Mexico, only to end up in El Salvador without any money to get back home. Francisco stayed there for two years. When he was twelve, Francisco journeyed to Guatemala and then to Mexico. He spent two years living off the streets and begging. Finally, a woman took him in, and her husband agreed to teach Francisco to be a mechanic. Before long he was on his way again, and this time he made it to the border town of Reynosa, Mexico.

Francisco almost drowned in the Rio Grande, so he returned to the Mexican side determined to find a safer crossing place. On the next try he made it across

south of McAllen, Texas. He traveled to Houston by train, but when he found no help there he boarded another train, this time to Harlingen and then on to Brownsville, in south Texas. Again, he found no help, so he returned to Harlingen starving and exhausted. In desperation, Francisco tried to flag down the border patrol, but the officers were involved in chasing other "illegals" at the time, and they ignored him. Eventually, the border patrol agents did catch up with Francisco, and they placed him in a home for unaccompanied minors.

Now, Francisco wants to become a mechanic and a U.S. citizen, to be married, and to help the people who helped him in his flight from Nicaragua.

EDUARDO

Eduardo is the oldest of six children. He lived in Guatemala, but at sixteen he found himself consumed by fear of the military. And with good reason. Many of his friends had been "recruited" by being dragged off the streets.

A fifty-mile bus ride put him in Mexico, but there he was mugged and all of his money was stolen. He had no choice but to live on the streets for a few weeks, surviving on a series of day jobs that paid little.

He walked all the way to the U.S. border, crossed it easily, but then found neither work nor a place to sleep. Eventually he was caught in the Rio Grande Valley by U.S. immigration officers.

Eduardo lies awake at night, lonely and hoping that someday he will be reunited with his family.

*A map on the wall of a home for unaccompanied
minors. Children have torn off pieces of the border-
lands they traversed.*

TRAPPED!—DETENTION CENTERS

Port Isabel Service Processing Center is a holding facility located in a bleak spot about twenty-five miles east of Harlingen, Texas, on the Gulf of Mexico. But the center looks so much like a prison that the refugees call it *"El Coralon,"* which means a holding pen for people who've committed a crime and are awaiting sentencing. The center is enclosed by double lines of chain-link fence topped by barbed wire. The residents wear orange suits, and there are guards everywhere.

All the refugees at Port Isabel are at least eighteen years old. Husbands and wives are separated during their stay. On a typical day there are approximately one thousand men and three hundred women in residence, most of whom have been picked up at the airport and bus stations, known locally as the "combat zones."

Life in a detention center isn't very encouraging for these people who risked their lives coming to the United States in search of the American dream. They are roused early for a breakfast served at 5:30 A.M.. During the day, some of them have chores around the center, but most of them simply stay on their beds, talking, resting, playing games, or just waiting.

Some men are housed in tents that accommodate up to three hundred beds. The women stay in a building so crowded that the beds block the emergency exits—which were padlocked when we were there. Privacy is unthinkable.

There are very few lawyers available to the detainees. Often their "private" meeting with a lawyer means that fifty people, most of whom speak no English, are placed in a room with one lawyer!

And sadly, about 95 percent of the people held in a detention center are deported.

The detention center is a jail-like facility where
single adults are detained, even though
technically they have committed no crime.

A holding station for prisoners as they wait to be escorted back to their quarters at the end of a day.

Upon arriving at a detention center, a refugee's belongings are put into a small box and tagged with his name and registration number. This box is held until it is time for the refugee to leave.

Pay phones are available to the detainees. However, most of them don't know anyone they can telephone for help.

Overleaf:
This tent is a typical accommodation for men within a detention center. Depending on the number of refugees apprehended, additional tents may be pitched.

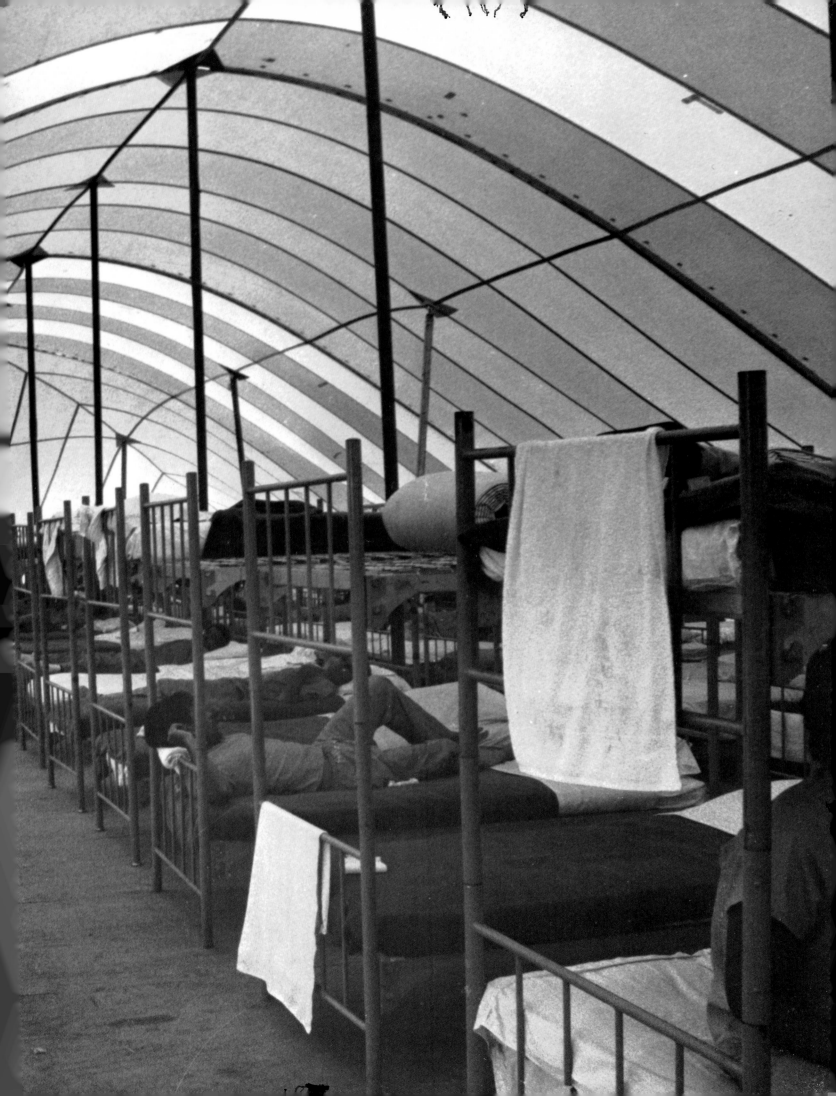

A man sits alone by one of the tents in the detention center. Privacy is hard to come by, and there is nowhere detainees can hide to escape reality.

All that those who stay in a detention center can do is wait. It seems that their futures are in the hands of arbitrary forces.

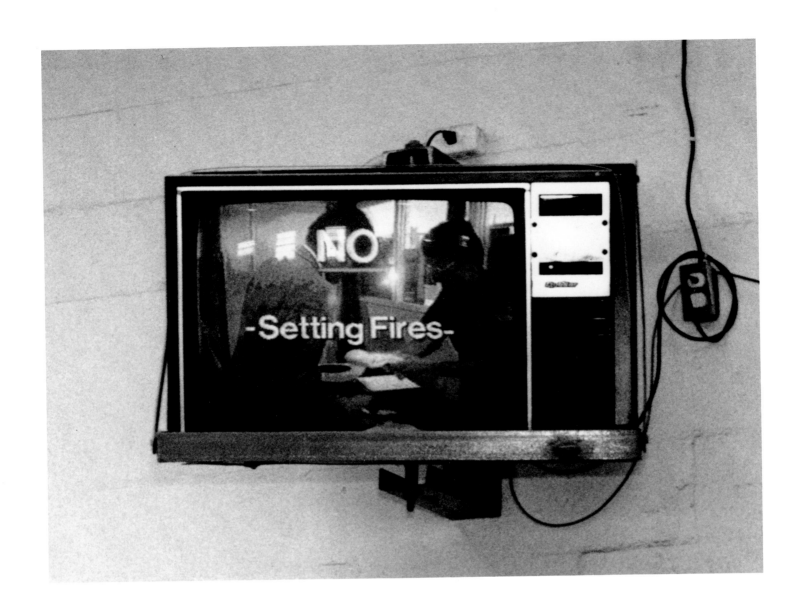

The women, in contrast to the men, are housed
indoors. They are all required to wear orange
uniforms, too. In the women's quarters, television
monitors continuously display the center's rules.

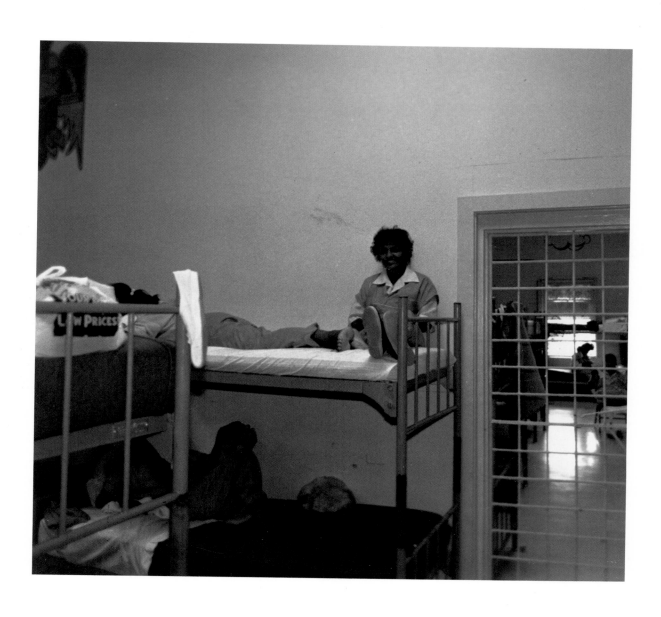

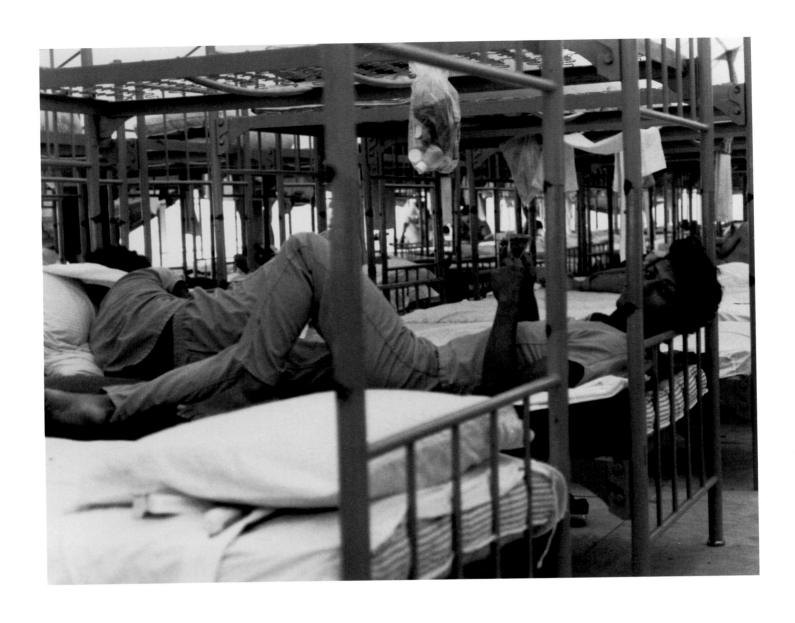

Even husbands and wives are segregated by sex.
Housed in separate accommodations, spouses
never see each other.

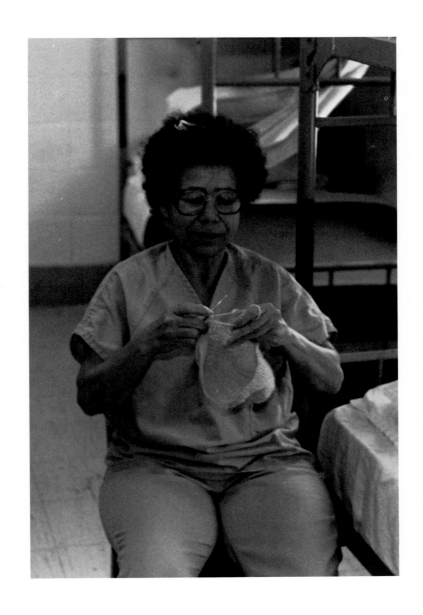

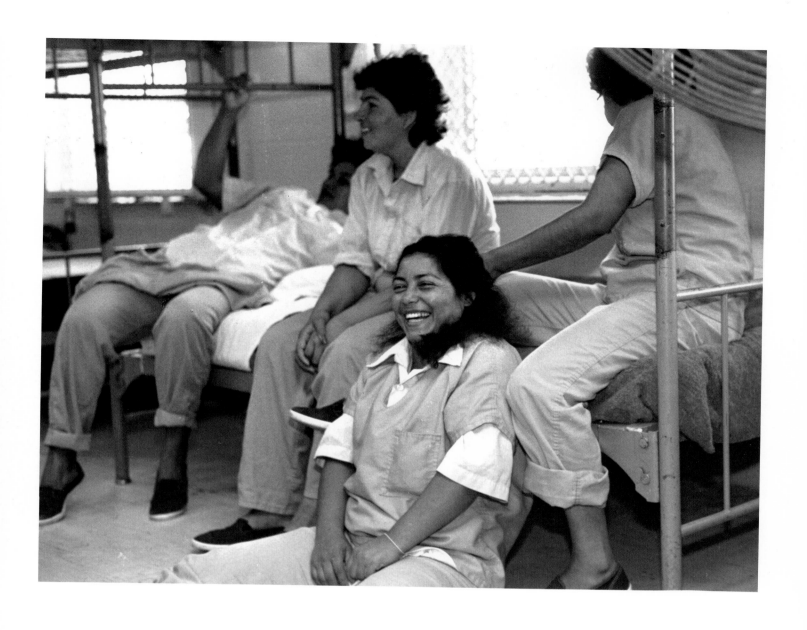

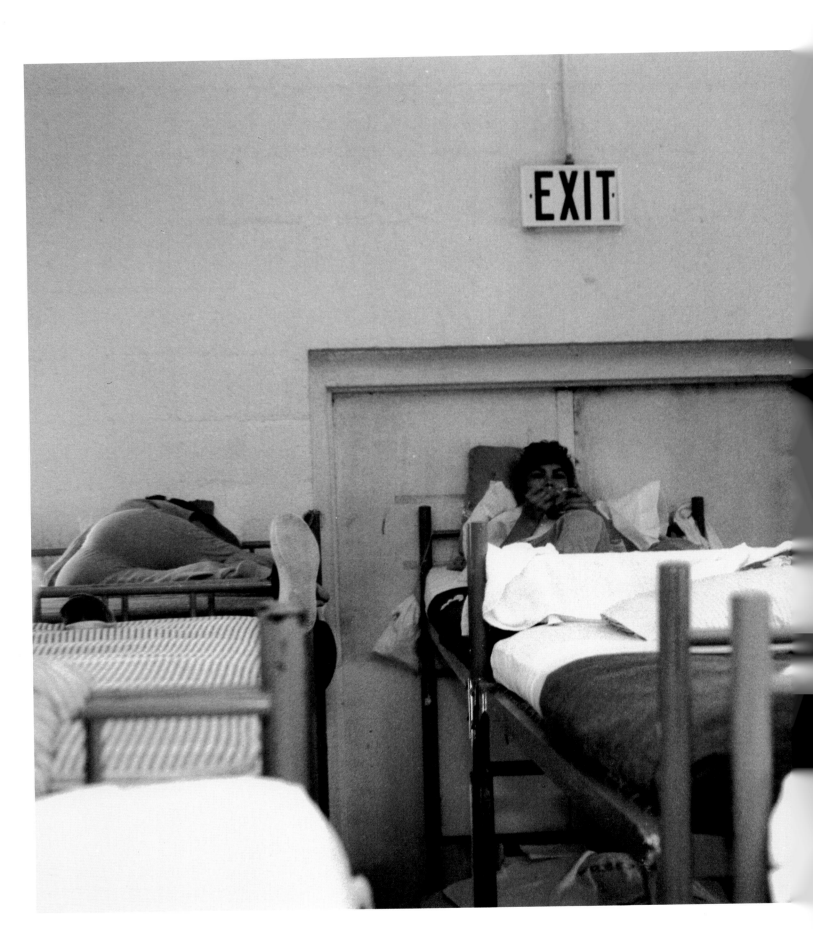

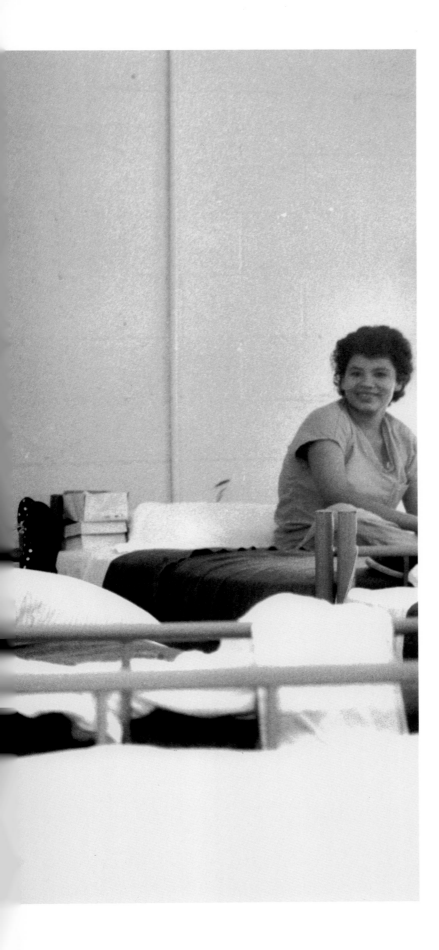

There are so many bunk beds in this women's building that they even block the emergency exit—an obvious fire hazard.

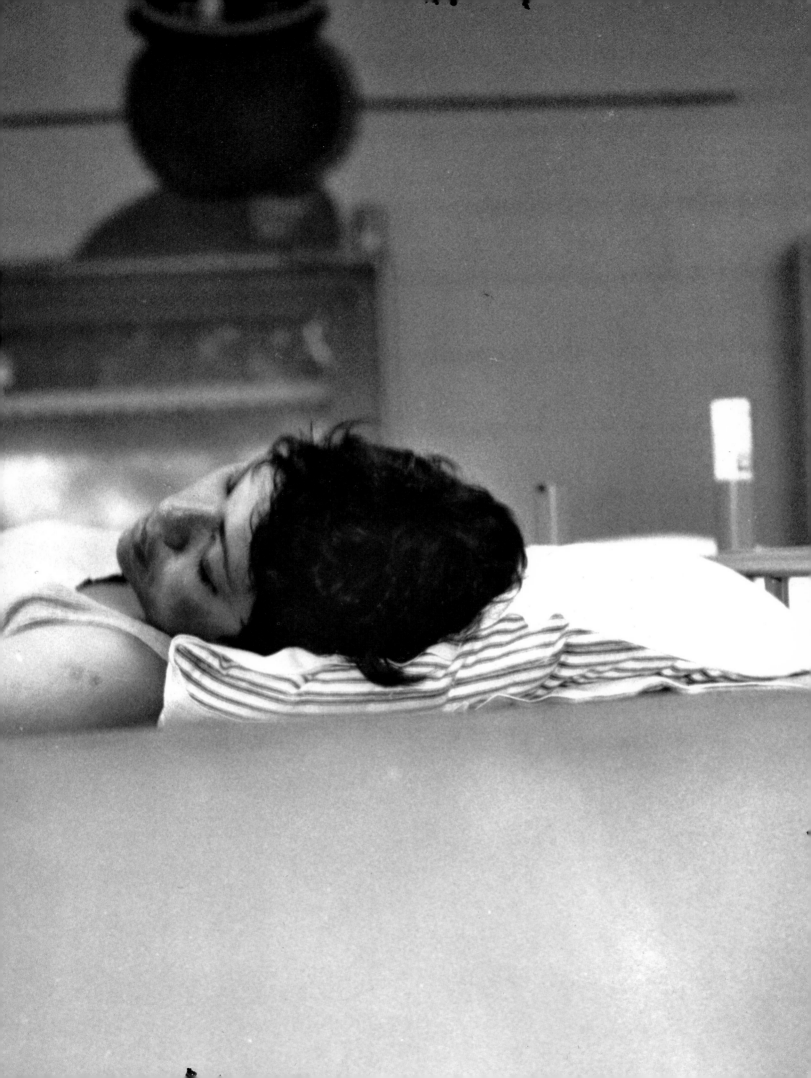

SHELTERS—WHERE THE RED CROSS SHINES

The Red Cross shelters are *not* detention facilities. Rather, they are holding stations for the "illegals" until the INS decides where they will go. The residents are free to leave whenever they want, but most have nowhere to go. Primarily, the shelters house families; we saw very few unaccompanied aliens. The average stay ranges from one to eight weeks. Most of the residents come from Central America, but even families from Poland have signed themselves in. We learned that it is not uncommon to find Asians and Eastern Europeans trying to enter the United States through south Texas. Many of these people first flee to Mexico and then try to enter the United States.

The refugees at the Red Cross shelter in San Benito are housed in rooms as large as airplane hangars. They sleep on cots, their belongings piled beside them. They frequently spend the day on their cots, though there are some activities. English is taught to anyone who is interested, and many of the children tried out their newly learned words on us. For younger children there is even a classroom. At the time of our visit there were more than three hundred families in residence, so the food lines were long, the portions scanty. A deportation office and an INS officer are on the grounds.

The Brownsville Red Cross Shelter has a greater number of occupants because of it's larger facility and proximity to the border. There were more than seven hundred families when we visited, making for extremely crowded conditions. The residents live in small shacks furnished with cots. Despite the crush of people, the shelter seems to work well, and we left with the impression that the staff tries hard to help the "illegals."

Of course, the threat of being deported immediately does not hang over the families who live in these shelters. They appear cheerful and certainly not without hope—in marked contrast to the residents of the detention centers.

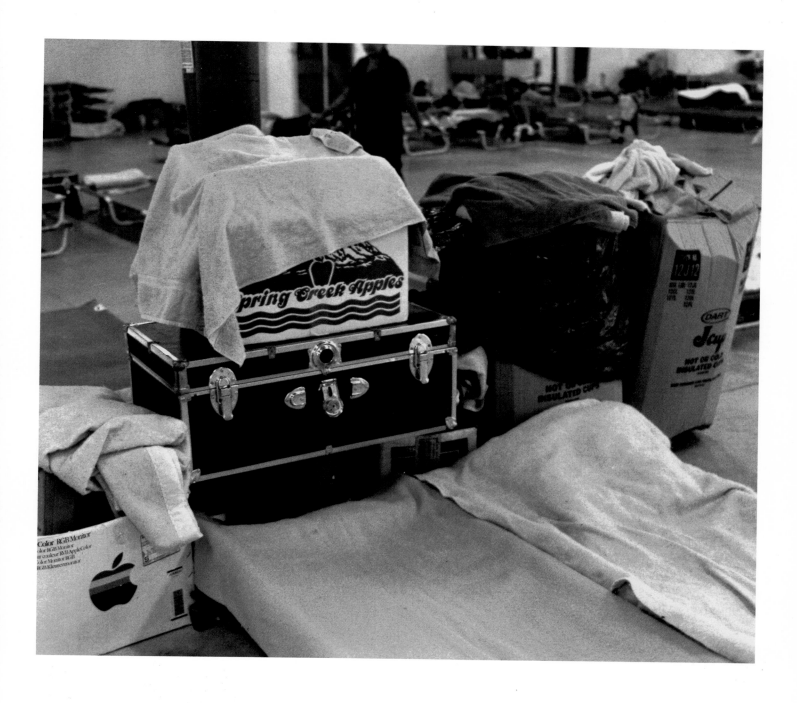

All "illegals" who come to the Red Cross shelters are registered. They are free to leave at any time, but most stay for prolonged periods. Until their immigration applications are considered, they have nowhere to go, there are no jobs available, and their children are not allowed to attend the local schools.

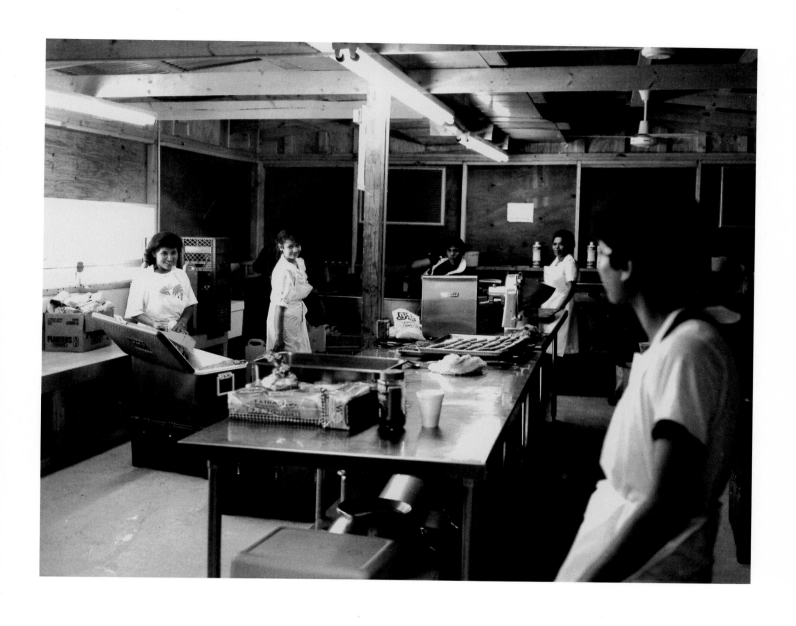

Chores are shared at the shelters, and the refugees themselves cook the meals.

January 1989 — Brownsville Shelter

Date	# of Shelters	Individuals Sheltered	Today Meals	Meals to Date
9	4	370	370	370
10	5	369	738	1108
11	5	519	1095	2203
12	3	235	730	2933
13	3	240	685	3618
14	1	169	997	4615
15	1	232	868	5483
16	1	296	1144	6627
17	1	315	1620	8247
18	1	290	1133	9380
19	1	274	1146	10,526
20	1	247	899	11,425
21	1	244	1035	12,460
22	1	254	962	13,422
23	1	260	1134	14,556
24	1	265	1168	15,724
25	1	255	1099	16,823
26	1	259	1422	18,245
27	1	252	1570	19,815
28	1	273	1393	21,208
29	1	301	1408	22,616
30	1	306	1445	24,061
31	1	293	1587	25,648

February, 1989 — Brownsville USDA Shelter

Date	Persons Sheltered	Meals today	Total Meals
1	282	1136	26,784
2	338	1667	28,451
3	308	1374	29,825
4	331	1671	31,496
5	334	1412	32,908
6	340	1486	34,394
7	336	1471	35,865
8	341	1617	37,482
9	359	1566	39,048
10	340	1452	40,500
11	433	1608	42,108
12	493	1983	44,091
13	565	2253	46,344
14	737	2310	48,654
15	567	2180	50,834
16	625	3722	54,556
17	627	2669	57,225
18	629	2672	59,897
19	509	2361	62,258
20	386	2149	64,407
21	497	1573	65,980
22	443	1871	67,851
23	420	2312	70,163
24	532	2096	72,259
25	557	2088	74,347
26	594	2232	76,579
27	679	2074	78,653
28	711	2585	81,238

March, 1989 — Brownsville USDA Shelter

Date	Persons Sheltered	Meals Today	Meals to Date
1	762	2575	83,813
2	807	2580	86,393
3	760	2795	89,188
4	739	2840	92,028
5	861	2889	94,917
6	845	2712	97,629
7	847	2861	100,490
8	818	2864	103,354
9	883	2600	105,954
10	930	2782	108,736
11	915	3034	111,770
12	923	3102	114,872
13	922	2884	117,756
14	936	2835	120,591
15	926	2883	123,474
16	955	2999	126,473
17	981	3260	129,753
18	959	2861	132,594
19	981	2940	135,534
20	1024	2981	138,515
21	1052	3535	142,050
22	969	3725	145,775
23	1039	3066	148,841
24	1060	2772	151,613
25	1063	3311	154,924
26	1032	2894	157,818
27	1049	2767	160,585
28	1078	3040	163,625
29	1076	3295	166,920
30	1013	3100	170,020
31	1016	2748	172,768

At the Brownsville Red Cross Shelter a record of the number of individuals sheltered and the meals served is posted each day.

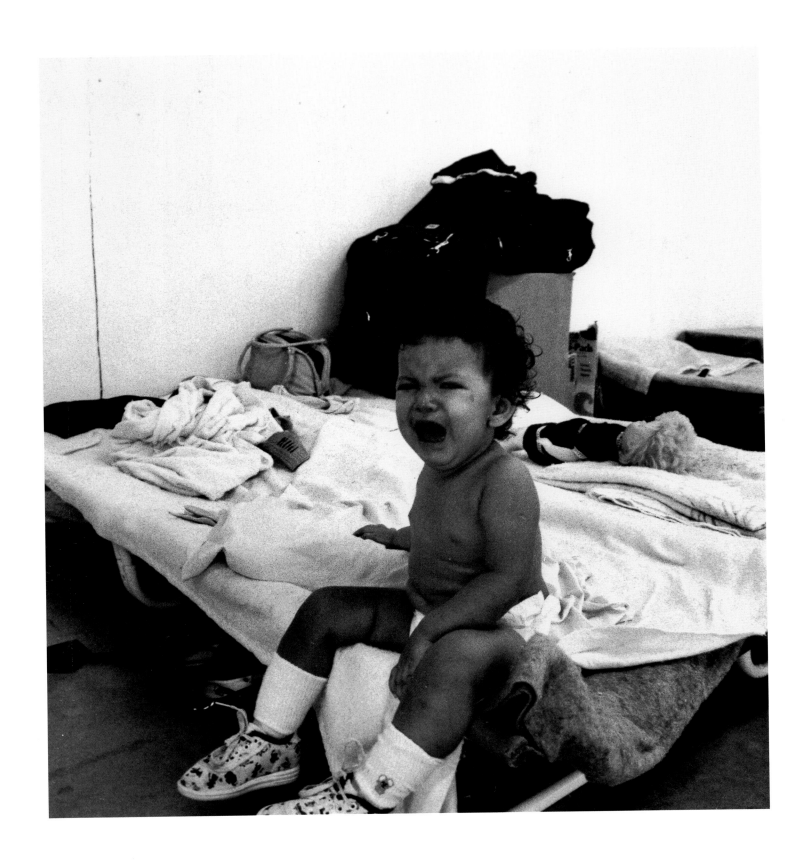

The young children are taught English at the Red Cross shelters. Many of these kids have had very little education in their own countries. If they are able to stay in the United States, knowing English will, of course, be very important.

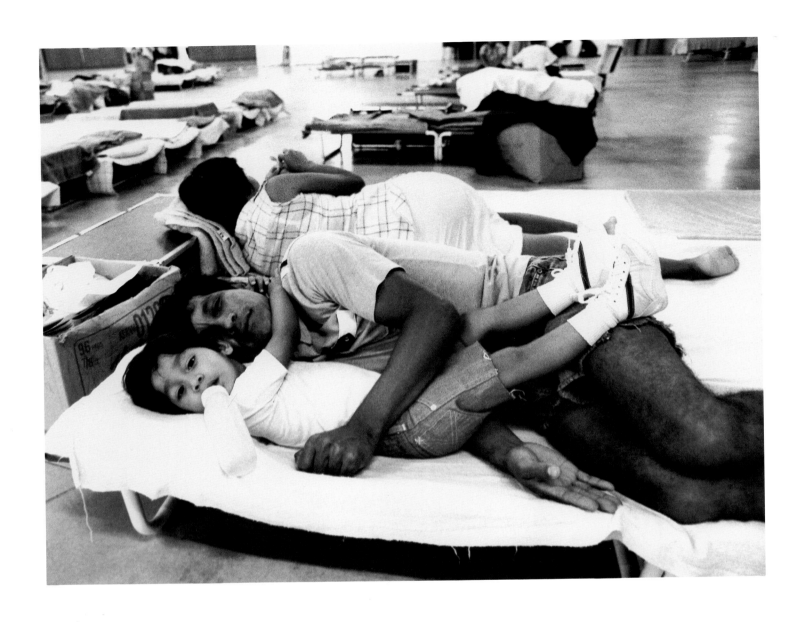

Many of the refugees at the shelters simply sit down and think, waiting to find out where they will go next. Others (overleaf) try to release their energy in organized activities.

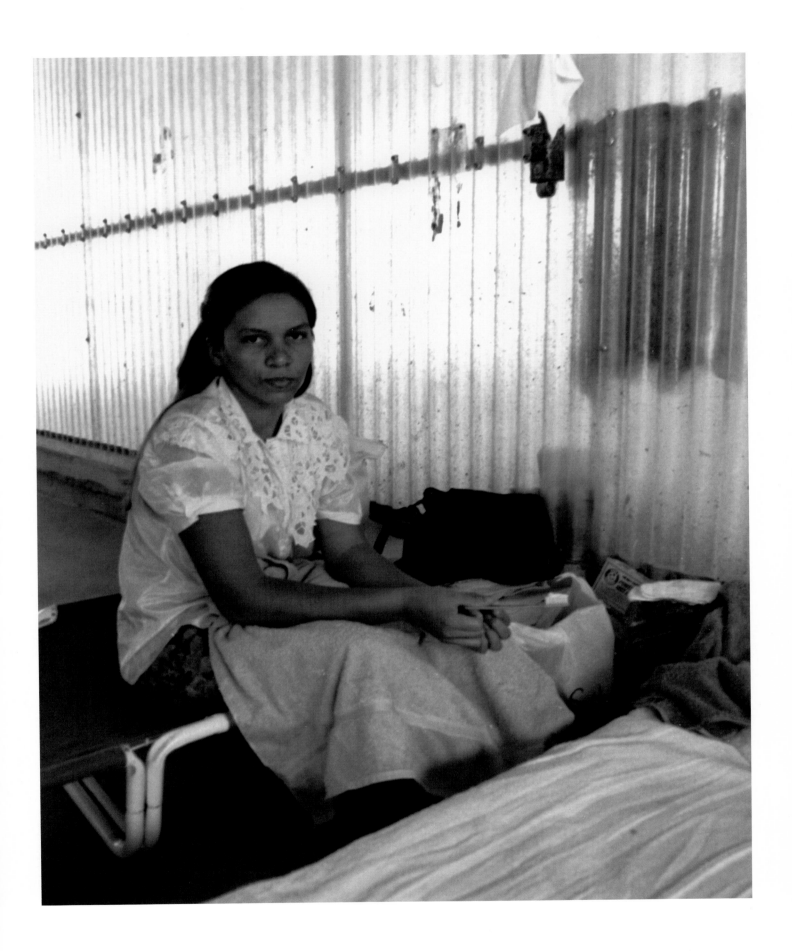

The Red Cross shelters house people of all ages. In many cases, an entire family, including grandparents, enters the United States together.

Everywhere in the Rio Grande Valley there is the problem of overcrowding. Families will go anywhere to be alone.

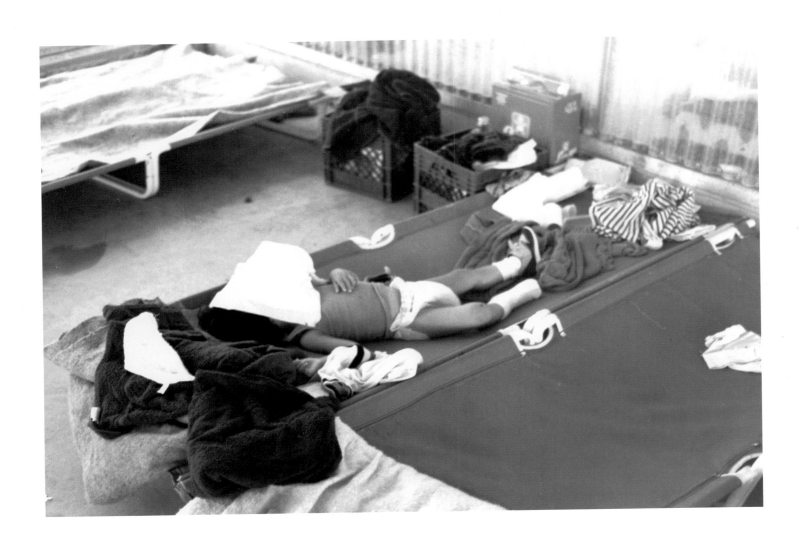

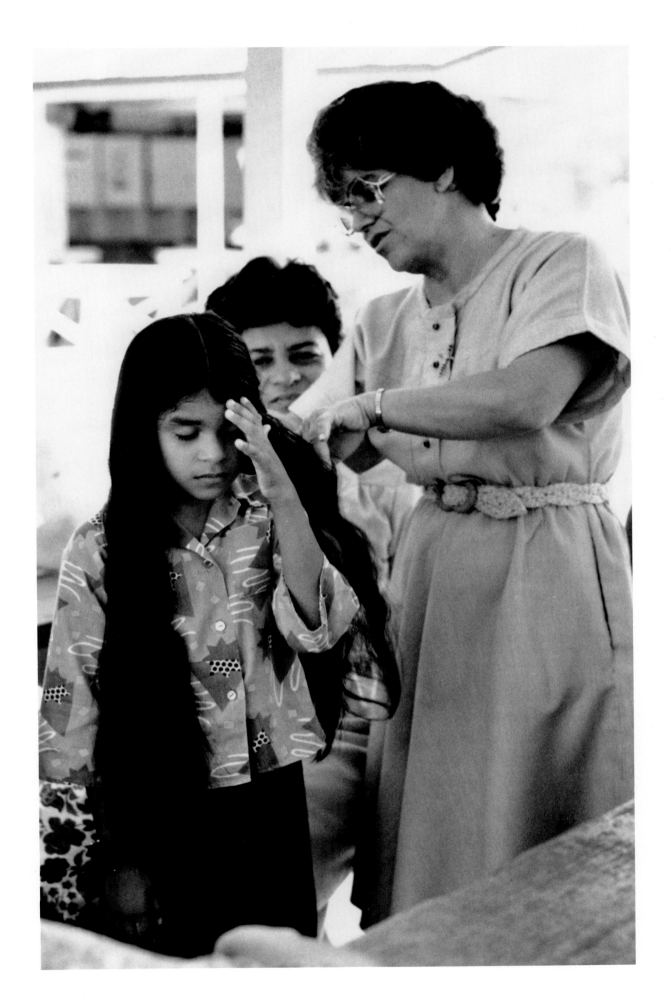

ACKNOWLEDGMENTS

Institutional

American Red Cross

Baer, Marks & Upham, New York

Border Association for Refugees of Central America

Brownsville Community Health Center, Texas

Brownsville Red Cross Shelter, Texas

Casa de Proyecto Libertad, Texas

Casa Oscar Romeo, Texas

Congressional Research Service

Eastman Kodak Company

Harrison, New York, Public Library

Home for Unaccompanied Minors, Los Fresnos, Texas

Immigration and Naturalization Service, Washington, D.C., and Texas

International Emergency Shelter, Raymondville, Texas

International Education Service

Minolta Corporation

Port Isabel Service Processing Center

Raymondville, Texas, International Emergency Shelter

San Benito Red Cross Shelter, Texas

SGI Graphics, Stamford, Connecticut

Time-Life Inc. (Photolab), New York

United States Border Patrol, Texas

United States Committee for Refugees, Washington, D.C.

United States Department of Justice
(Immigration and Refugee Affairs), Washington, D.C.

Individuals

Dan Benson

Robert Bothell

Hugh Brown

David Burke

Peter J. Christopoulos

Vittoria Di Palma

Giovannell Dunn

John Durniak

Alejandro Flores

Juan Garcia

Joe Garner

Scott Greenlee

Romon Guzman

Elizabeth Hock

Vern Jervis

Edward M. Kennedy,
United States Senator

David Hume Kennerly

Virginia Kice

Eric Martins

Charles Miers

Anne D. Miller

Daniel Perez

Lynn Raymond

Frank Riley

Maria Rodriguez

Chris Toal

David Travino

Jesse Villareal

James Walis

Ruth Wasem

Jeffrey L. Weiss

Robert A. Wooten

Roger Winter

*Special thanks to our families, in particular to
our fathers, Ernie Anastos and Dick French,
for their support and encouragement. Without
their faith in us and our abilities this book
would never have been possible.*
P.A.   C.F.

"America is a passionate belief in freedom and in the worth and dignity of human personality. We must not let the song die on our lips."

Harry Emerson Fosdick